Good-bye my Fancy

WITH WALT WHITMAN IN HIS LAST DAYS

WITH WALT WHITMAN IN HIS LAST DAYS

Judith Grace

Ulysses Books
Oregon House, CA
2003

Published by Ulysses Books
Oregon House, CA
www.ulyssesbooks.com

Good-bye My Fancy

With Walt Whitman in His Last Days
Copyright © 2003 Judith Grace

FIRST EDITION

Book design: Stefano Landini.

Cover photo: Oscar Lion Collection, rare books, The New York Public Library. Other photos: Courtesy Library of Congress.

Printed on acid-free paper

ISBN 0-9645782-6-3

Manufactured in the United States of America

Library of Congress Cataloging-in-Publication Data
Grace, Judith.
Good-bye, my fancy: with Walt Whitman in his last days / by Judith Grace.-- 1st ed.
p. cm.
ISBN 0-9645782-6-3 (paperback: alk. paper)
1. Whitman, Walt, 1819-1892--Drama. 2. Traubel, Horace, 1858-1919--Drama. 3. Camden (N.J.)--Drama. 4. Aged men--Drama. 5. Poets--Drama. I. Title.
PS3607.R326G66 2003
812'.6--dc22
2003022317

Camarado, this is no book,
Who touches this touches a man.

Walt Whitman

CONTENTS

INTRODUCTION

The dialogue in these pages is a dialogue of truth. The conversations were real conversations, the situations and emotions real situations and emotions, even much of the physical actions described actually took place. The poetic license is minimal, while the poetry of the moments portrayed is as full as we could ask of the simple hours of any of our own days.

Good-bye My Fancy is a dramatization of the four years of conversation that took place between Walt Whitman and his young friend, secretary and literary executor, Horace Traubel, at Whitman's home in Camden, New Jersey. These conversations, recorded by Traubel and gathered together with many anecdotes, reminiscences, and letters that he eagerly collected and preserved, appear in full in *With Walt Whitman in Camden*, a nine-volume work (Horace anticipated eight volumes) that appeared a book at a time over a rather elongated ninety years, 1906 to 1996 – the last volume appearing seventy-seven years after its author's death. We could say that *Camden* is the story of two friends who enjoyed each other's company. But it is more accurate to say that the book relates two different stories: the last years, trials and death of our greatest American poet, as seen through the eyes of his close friend; and the experiences and eventual loss that so deeply influenced and shaped the future of a young writer and socialist thinker.

Horace, so it seems, began his massive work with the aim of faithfully recording as much as he could recall of Whitman's conversation during his evening visits to Mickle Street, and at weekend dinners and other events where he and Whitman were together. Whitman was not aware of Horace's daily notations. He knew that Horace would write about him, he wanted the young man to speak for him after he was gone. But Horace went him one better, by reproducing not only the words, but the tone, drift, hesitations, repetitions, staccato declamations, and colloquial quirks that comprised Whitman's private speech. Gertrude Traubel, Horace's daughter and the transcriber of Volumes 5 and 6, relates her mother's description of how he worked:

"The notes of the visits to Whitman were written on small bits of paper to fit into the pocket of his jacket and were written in what he called 'condensed longhand,' in the dim light of Whitman's room. Within the hour of the words spoken, the material was put into the complete form with which you are familiar in the three published volumes. There was no vacuum of time or emotion, thus preserving the vitality of the original conversation."

As such we have much more than a laundry list of sayings and aphorisms. We have the moment relived – Whitman reflective, annoyed, giddy, distracted, or just hungry. And we have him at all times speaking freely and frankly, unaware that posterity was sitting in the orchestra pit. We have clear, unsentimental descriptions of the feeble frame making its way across the room or lying exhausted on his bed. We have unexpected visits, unanticipated changes in events, sudden grumblings between the two friends that just as quickly resolve into renewed exchanges of friendship, in short, the many simple things that make up a daily life. This, we know, no formal biography could ever give us. We see of what an old man's life had consisted, and we see that this man more than passes the test of our respect. True greatness must be measured in the use we make of our many simple moments, and Whitman has much to teach us here. We can also say that, with Traubel's *Camden*, the poet was privileged to leave behind a second great work, to stand proudly alongside his beloved *Leaves of Grass*, no less than we look to *Conversations with Goethe* with as much reverence as *Faust*.

In *Good-bye My Fancy*, Ms. Grace provides us with a distillation in three simple, sometimes humorous, and always poignant scenes of the many, many nights that Horace and Walt passed together. Read this dialogue and enter thereby into the world that was 328 Mickle Street in those years. Here is Walt savoring the fresh air surrounding his young friend as he enters. Horace picking his way amid the litter to find a place to sit. Whitman struggling with his half-paralyzed body to move about the room, and struggling further with his weak lungs to carry forward the emotions and insights that Horace furtively committed to paper. Then there is the talk of the day, the business of getting the next book through the press, the news concerning their friends and acquaintances; those precious letters, photographs, and memoranda that Walt passed on piecemeal over the four years, for Horace to add to his "archive"; Horace reading an old letter back to Walt, and Walt listening and reminiscing; Walt complaining of his pains, or the smart of some recent criticism, and Horace rallying him once again. How much is here condensed! And then always, the affirming and reaffirming of their close bond of friendship.

Many readers will know that Whitman was not one to recite his own poetry, not even in private. As he himself told Horace, "I cannot remember a single line." But as this dialogue must portray the inner being that was Walt Whitman, so there is dramatized the fruits of that being. The poetry and the life were not separate; Whitman lived it thus, and Horace Traubel made sure the world knew it.

There is throughout this dialogue the inevitable thread of the gradual physical decline that Whitman suffered. It is right that this be portrayed, since this was the long, terrible trial of Whitman's final years. Day by day he witnessed a gradual decline. A reader new to *Camden* may feel at a first reading that the old man was in a perpetual stew of self-pity; but eventually one comes to realize – and Traubel also explicates it for us – that Whitman was simply watching it take place and speaking honestly about what he saw. The courage of this objective view of a man's own deterioration hits home when, in the last months of Whitman's life, he firmly admonished those who claimed that he would rise and walk again to compose new verses. Even the blunt Dr. Bucke, when he bid Whitman his last farewell, could not get past the sentiment of "until next time", only to have Walt lovingly repeat, "No, Maurice, you will never see me again." Horace knew the end would come, it was one of the great motivations for his daily vigilance and literary constancy. But the moment, when it arrived, was not without its days of deep sorrow and loss that nothing could replace.

Horace may have started out with the simple aim of writing down Whitman's words, but as the months pass, the fleeting glimpses of the amanuensis that *Camden* first gives us develop into a more complete portrait of a young man on a mission. By the time we reach the final twelve-month period of Whitman's life, we have a great deal of Horace himself, with his errands, conversations with friends and associates, and private thoughts. The need to nurture and expand the growing Whitman circle gradually presented Horace Traubel with a line of duties that he could not, and certainly had no wish to, shun, as he oversaw the printing of the final "Deathbed" edition of *Leaves of Grass*, maintained his and Walt's correspondence with friends and admirers all over Europe and America, and managed the care of his dying friend, which led to several daily visits, morning, noon and night, until the last inevitable moment arrived.

With all that *With Walt Whitman in Camden* has to give us, we must also say that it retains its own secrets, and *Good-bye My Fancy* keeps the secrets intact. We do not often hear of Horace's opinions of the other characters on the Mickle Street stage. And the reader must at times work hard to understand the dynamic of Traubel and Whitman's own interactions. Horace was eager to drink in whatever the poet had to say, but Horace did not always like what he heard. He would often let Whitman know this, though sometimes he seemed to do it in a rather surreptitious way, as though persuading the old man to complete Traubel's and not Whitman's thought. Despite this, of course, it is a tribute to their friendship that Traubel never gives one the impression of censoring or excising Whitman's words for the sake of decorum.

But finally, the most intriguing question of all is perhaps the one that would seem to have the most obvious answer: Why did he do it? Why write it all down, even the most innocuous remarks, every day for four years? Why? Friends do not do this for friends, which is no strike against friendship. There must have been something more, something so large and special that it would have been a crime for it to go unportrayed.

The answer, it would seem, was the being that was Walt Whitman. To Horace Traubel, Walt Whitman was not a famous writer. He was a man of incredible presence and disarming simplicity, a man who possessed a spiritual nature at once obvious and unfathomable to the person who witnessed it. Many visitors to that second floor bedroom have devoted much energy to describing the man and his unusual nature. Horace rarely did this, perhaps it never really occurred to him. What mattered was to get it down, to rescue as many of the moments of this man's life as he could possibly muster in twenty-four hours. We who read a hundred years hence are grateful.

Robert MacIsaac
Co-editor *With Walt Whitman in Camden*

A Dialogue in Three Parts

Persons of the Dialogue

Walt Whitman, the American poet, in his seventies
Horace Traubel, his secretary and friend, age thirty

The time of the dialogue covers the years 1890-1892, the last three years of Whitman's life. The entire action takes place in the bedroom of Walt Whitman's home in Camden, New Jersey.

PART I
About seven o'clock in the evening,
November 1890

It is evening; a fire is burning in the woodstove. WALT WHITMAN sits in a wicker rocking chair, next to a tall piano-stool gas-lamp, preparing a bundle. He is wearing a blue bathrobe and a gray hat. His feet are touching the stove; periodically he stirs the fire with a poker. A quilt lies across his knees; his cane leans against the chair. There is a cider jug, glasses, apples and a sherry bottle with flowers on the table.

The room is in great disorder: manuscripts, newspapers, clippings, letters, envelopes and photographs are strewn wildly over the table, floor and chairs, and overflow from boxes, baskets, and an open trunk. Memoranda are pinned to the tablecloth. Books are stacked all around. A half-written manuscript lies on the bed. A pen and open inkstand are on a small table nearby. A photograph of Lincoln is on the mantelpiece. A cage with a canary stands near the bed.

HORACE TRAUBEL enters.

WALT
Is that you Horace?
   (As Horace approaches, Walt greets him with outstretched hand)
Howdy! Howdy! Your hand is cold – it tempts me out of doors.
   (Horace hangs his hat on the bedpost)
But Horace! Is it hot here? And is it not cool out of doors?

What of the evening? Is it clear – beautiful – moonlighty?

HORACE
It's cold and clear outside.

WALT
Clear did you say? And do the stars shine? And the moon?
Is it a half moon? Oh! It must be one of God's perfect
nights!
  (Sighs, then motions toward the chair)
Got you seated.

HORACE
How have you been today, Walt? You don't look so well.

WALT
I do poorly, poorly. This has been as bad a day as any since
my sickness began – and I'm not sorry to say goodbye to
it. I had another of my spells – the worst so far.

HORACE
Walt! How did that happen?

WALT
I had undertaken to take a trip downstairs again alone.

HORACE
But the doctor said not to do that!

WALT

I had to do something to escape from my cell here. The stroke came without warning – so quickly I barely had time to lift and drop my cane. The sensation was one of total collapse – giving way – things getting out from under me. I fell to the floor and lay there several hours waiting for the cloud to pass.

HORACE

Why don't you listen to our warnings? Why don't you warn yourself?

WALT

I'll never again attempt to make the trip alone – never. I promise. It was a close call – a close call. I know my peril – it cannot be concealed. I have just about reached the end of my rope – the last strand has almost given out…

HORACE

I can't bring my heart to say amen to that!

WALT

Thank you boy. But the truth is today marks a new epoch in my life. Another stage on the downhill road.

HORACE

I shouldn't think with your idea of death you would speak of it as a downhill road!

WALT

Sure enough – the word was false. Uproad – up – up – another stage on the uphill road. That certainly sounds more like me, and I want to be like myself.

(Pause)

You know, that question came back to me in fifty different forms as I lay there footing up my accounts with the Almighty. We are not going to expect to lose even a losing fight – that would not be like us. We are not easily subdued. We must stick, eternally stick, until sticking itself will stick no more.

HORACE

Isn't it time we got you the wheelchair, Walt?

WALT

Going out at all now is out of the question. The mere navigation downstairs would be impossible.

HORACE

If only you could be outside wheeling along in the air, it would all come back to you at once!

WALT

Yes, I can see how that might be well. That was my old way. If anything went wrong I would get my stick and hobble down to the water – loll about in my favorite loafing places – the rivers, the wharves, the boats – see the boys at the ferries…

HORACE
You just say the word and we will get the chair and fix the rest of it.

WALT
Oh, do you say that?
  (Pause, then excitedly)
I think we might try it boy!
  (Motioning)
I want a back up this high to rest my head on –

HORACE
I saw one just like that in the catalogue!

WALT
Well, I do not object to plainness – no cushions – wicker-bottom – something like this –
  (Taps his rocking chair)
and solid.

HORACE
And liberal in size.

WALT
Yes, that undoubtedly. But that will come about easily. Most of the users of these chairs are old plugs like me – broad at the beam – who won't be squeezed down at their time of life.

HORACE

Walt, just think how much good it will do you to be wheeling out and around the corner!

WALT

Ah yes – get a sniff of the great outdoors! Oh! The joy of that! And the greater joy after a while of getting to the ferry! And greatest joy of all, getting wheeled to the boat! Oh! That will so intoxicate me, I'll want to jump overboard!

(The canary begins to warble)

That's my canary bird – cheeriest of birds! We need but a snake – then our menagerie will be complete.

(After a thoughtful pause)

Come over here, Horace.

(Horace goes over and takes Walt's hand)

I seem every day to be losing something – some atom of power. If I get another blow like the one today, where would it leave me? Way up on the shore probably. It's time we were thinking of bringing out the book – the complete works – don't you think? I am reckoning upon you to help me before I light out – indeed I cannot bring it out very well if you say no. I am depending upon your good will – your love – to stick by me for this job. We ought to make a good team working together. I could do little or nothing alone. It won't be for long anyhow.

(Horace says nothing, only presses Walt's hand; Walt laughs merrily)

I knew you would say yes.

HORACE
You know now Walt, I am at your command – ready, willing, anxious to serve you.

WALT
Yes, and I shall call on you.

HORACE
You believe all this of me?

WALT
Yes – I do my boy. I know you. I believe you.

HORACE
And maybe that book will finally bring you some money?

WALT
What do I need with money anyhow. I have enough. A few dollars more or less – what do they amount to?

HORACE
A few dollars more means a great deal if you ain't got 'em!

WALT
I should say, and don't I know! Hasn't my prosperity walked on its uppers almost from the start!

HORACE

I suppose the book will be a dollar and a half?

WALT

No – that's too much. Not more than a dollar and a quarter at the most – a dollar if possible. I like to keep my prices down at the level of my real friends. The people with money wouldn't buy me anyhow. Leaves of Grass is a book for the criminal classes.

HORACE

How do you make that out?

WALT

I don't make it out – it is the fact. The other people do not need a poet.

HORACE

Are you in the criminal class yourself?

WALT

Yes, certainly. Why not?

HORACE

Let me in!

WALT

Day by day, in these older years of my life, I see how lucky

I was that I was myself thrown out early upon the average earth. I was, in a sense, a boy of the farm and the streets. It was my fate, my good fate. After all, if a fellow is to write poetry, the secret is – get in touch with humanity – know what the people are thinking about – retire to the very deepest sources of life – back, back, till there is no farther point to retire to.

HORACE
Walt, Doctor Bucke calls Leaves of Grass Whitman's bible.

WALT
Whitman's bible, eh? God help you!

HORACE
The gospel is spreading!

WALT
Yes, as fire once started in the grass. It is a new experience to be successful. I always seem to know what to do with failure, but success is a puzzle for me. It is very interesting, that just as I am about to step out, I am like to be applauded... You can have no idea of the bitterness of the feeling against me in those early days. I was a tough – obscene. Leaves of Grass was taboo – prosecuted as an indecent book – banned from the bookstores – kept in the libraries under lock and key so it might not get out and be read.
(Fervently)

Will the world ever get over its own indecencies and stop attributing them to God? The poems – Children of Adam – are very innocent. Yet I have heard nothing but expurgate, expurgate, expurgate from the day I started.

HORACE
If you accepted all the suggestions there wouldn't be one leaf of the Leaves left...

WALT
Well that's the truth, even if you do say it!
　　(Puts on glasses, ruffles through a copy of Leaves of Grass on the table)
What do you think, Horace? I really got put through fire for this one:
　　(Reads)
"Hair, bosom, hips, bend of legs, negligent falling hands all diffused, mine too diffused,
Ebb stung by the flow and flow stung by the ebb, love-flesh swelling and deliciously aching,
Limitless limpid jets of love hot and enormous, quivering jelly of love, white blow and delirious juice,
Bridegroom night of love working surely and slowly into the prostrate dawn,
Undulating into the willing and yielding day,
Lost in the cleave of the clasping and sweet-flesh'd day."
　　(Looks up)
Now is that something to shake a house down?

HORACE

Nothing but plain facts – plain divine facts.

WALT

Mighty changes are coming, Horace – are soon to come – when the whole affair of sex will be treated with the respect to which it is entitled. Instead of meaning shame and being apologized for, it will mean purity and will be glorified. Sex – sex – sex! Whether you sing or make a machine, or go to the North Pole, or love your mother, or build a house, black shoes – or anything – anything at all – it's sex – sex – sex! Sex is the root of all – sex – the coming together of men and women – sex – sex! –

HORACE

(Breaking in)

And marriage? What of marriage?

WALT

I don't know about marriage. But about love – well love will always take care of itself.

HORACE

And free love?

WALT

Why, are you catechizing me? Free love? Is there any other kind of love?

(Pause)

A man was here the other day who asked me, "Don't you feel rather sorry on the whole you wrote the sex poems?" I answered by asking him another question, "Don't you feel rather sorry on the whole that I am Walt Whitman?" Wasn't that rich?...

(Remembering)

I remember a woman too. Broke in on me years ago, one day when I was alone – downstairs – at the window, where I used to sit so much. She came in innocently enough, talked for a while innocently enough, then suddenly broke loose on Children of Adam – on me— giving us hell from A to Z. I was surprised, almost scared.

HORACE
Well – how did it end?

WALT
She accused me of a deliberate desire to ruin boys, girls, people by my flagrant philosophy – went on in that strain.

HORACE
Did you answer her any?

WALT
Not a word – I never said a word.

HORACE

How did it end up?

WALT

My silence seemed to astonish her. "Haven't you a single thing to say in your own defense?" she finally asked me. I said, "Madam, I need no defense. I only need to be understood." That mystified her. She said, "No one would suppose, Walt Whitman, from looking at you that you are the sort of man your books show you to be." She didn't intend that for a compliment but I enjoyed it as such. Finally seeing she could make no impression, that I was not inclined to debate with her, she withdrew. I said quietly, "Come again."

(Pause)

So you see, Horace, things do happen, some things, now and then, even here, in this Quaker household.

(Pouring cider)

Here is some cider. I want you to drink it with me. It tastes very genuine – is very much appley.

HORACE

I've just had supper.

WALT

Oh! This will do you good even if you have!

(Pause)

For a long time all I got out of my work was the work

itself and a few amens. I was not only not popular, but I was non grata – not welcome in the world at any price. Now and then a man steps back from the crowd – says, "I will be myself" – does because he is – something immense. The howl that goes up is tremendous. Some step back. Some stay and go on.

HORACE
You stayed and went on!

WALT
Well, I hope so. I hope so. Leaves of Grass stands not for pleasant facts only, but fact, all tempests, horrors, hoggishnesses, Judas Iscariots – everything – whatever. It's no wonder it brought the whole pack – literary men, editors, politicians, priests – howling at my heels: down Walt Whitman – drive him into obscurity, hurry him into oblivion… I wonder I never did anything violent with the book it so victimized me!

HORACE
Ha! Ha! The poor victim is still making books even at the age of seventy-one.

WALT
It does seem rather laughable, don't it? But the truth is, what for hard knocks, I haven't a whole bone left in my body. I had dozens of such rubs if I had two…

(Pause)

There was a nobleman came over here with a letter of introduction to me from some man of high standing in England – William Rossetti. There was a fancy dinner in Cambridge with many of the swell fellows present. The man I speak of was the principal guest. In the course of their dinner he mentioned the letter to me. Lowell – the poet – who had had a couple of glasses of wine – was flushed – called out, "What, a letter for Walt Whitman! For God Almighty's sake don't deliver it! Walt Whitman! Do you know who Walt Whitman is? Why Walt Whitman is a rowdy, a New York tough, a loafer, a frequenter of low places – a friend of cab drivers!" The note was never delivered.

HORACE
(Searching through the papers strewn on Walt's floor, he finds an old article and shows it to Walt)
What's this, Walt?

WALT
That's a curio, Horace – an article from the Philadelphia Press. Don't it beat the whole world for telling the truth, the whole truth, nothing but the truth?

HORACE
(Reads)
"There may be something interesting in Whitman's

personality, as there is undoubtedly something pathetic in his poverty – but we have always failed to comprehend the interest in his poetry – we call it such by courtesy. If Walt Whitman were what his admirers' defective sense of style fancies him, he would be expressive."

WALT
Let him go to hell – that's all I have for him!

HORACE
That's expressive anyway!

WALT
The Press has been the meanest, most malignant, most lying – a searcher after hidden blacknesses, a suspicioner of motives, a pecker at the foibles of humanity – a sort of journalistic imp of a Beelzebub!

HORACE
Hasn't it stimulated you after all? It brought the red back into your face...

WALT
That's certainly a cheerful way to look at it, Horace. I may after all have something even to thank the Press for.
  (Laughs tiredly)
I get mad at people, then people get mad at me. That's the way we even up.

(Throws the article into the stove; Horace makes a gesture in protest)

You don't know, Horace, what a good investment this new stove has been. I take a few articles, poke them in, put logs on top of them, apply a match – then, the fire is here! I know you are jealous of that fire!

(Pause)

Don't think I blame 'em. No story is complete without the slaps as well as the kisses. Besides, it's best not to have a royal road. It stiffens a fellow up to be told all around that he is not wanted, that his room is better than his company, that he has a good heart – that he can nurse soldiers, but can't write poetry.

HORACE

But you got into the magazines some – you were received here and there – you didn't have any more fight to go through than any rebel must expect to encounter. Why should you growl?

WALT

I don't. Did you ever hear me growl?

HORACE

A little. Sometimes. Yes.

WALT

Is that so? Then I take the growl back. A man who

proposes something new and will not give people time to see it is not worthy of his message.

HORACE
After all – did you care what the world thought of you?

WALT
Yes, I cared – but not enough to give up my fight.
(Walt walks slowly over to the window, taking hold of the bed and table on the way)

HORACE
Can I help you, Walt?

WALT
No, I want to prove to you fellows I'm not completely gone up the spout.
(He arrives at the window)
I'm a slow arriver. I get there – but I always come in last.
(He opens the window, takes a deep breath and looks outside)
Look, Horace, the tops of the trees!
(Slowly he returns to his chair)
I don't seem to be worth my weight in feathers! God bless my chair! Well here I am. Or rather – here are my remains! But what's the use of complaining? Why should I trouble you with my pains? You have pains of your own.
(Horace says nothing)
I don't believe you have any pains of your own. I believe

you are a sickless animal. I don't believe you know what it is to be on your back.

HORACE
I don't actually.

WALT
Neither did I for the most of my life. I hardly knew I had a stomach or a head for all the trouble I had with either. In my case it started here twenty years ago –
(Indicating the back of his neck)
when I contracted blood poisoning dressing the wounds of a young soldier during the war. The effect on me was slow. It came down the whole side, arm, leg, face – led to a stroke in '73 – from which I never fully recovered. Luckily the stroke did not affect my power of speech, or my brain. Only my power to locomote, to get about was gone – or partly gone. I have seen the iron collars on the slaves in the South – bits on the wrist here, a chain – back of the collar a spike. The effect of all not pain, not anguish, but a dull weight – making its wearer incapable of effort – bearing him down. It is such a collar I wear day by day – a burden impossible to shake off. Now, Horace, you are my arms and my legs.

HORACE
I am not doing anything for you. I am doing everything for me.

WALT

(He looks fixedly at Horace)

I see what you mean, Horace; that is the right way to look at it. People used to say to me – Walt, you are doing miracles for those fellows in the hospitals. I wasn't. I was, as you would say, doing miracles for myself, that was all.

(Pause)

Horace, you tell the doctors not to worry – I do not worry. Tell them we are working out a job together and that I have promised not to die until the work is done. That should satisfy even the doctors.

(He reaches over and puts a new log in the stove)

There, Mr. Log, I have been preserving you just for this moment – now show what you can do!

(While getting the log, he knocks over his scrapbook on the floor)

HORACE

Walt! You musn't forget yourself and use this scrapbook for kindling!

WALT

No indeed. That's too precious, too useful. It has been about me now for fifty years. I am very close to it. It is one of my bibles. It is full of its beginnings – it is the ABC of Leaves of Grass – contains the first lisps of the song.

HORACE

It won't seem so important if it gets kicked about the floor a few more years.

WALT

That's sure enough. These things should be put in some secure place. I'll put them away, see that they don't drift onto the floor again.

HORACE

Don't destroy anything! These things – seeing them – having them – give your friends great joy.

WALT

When you put it that way I accept it. For a long time I had a little pen-knife that belonged, they told me, to Lincoln. I lost it. I felt as bad as if a dear friend had died.

(Pause)

Take anything that you choose, our partnership involves it. There is a sort of apostolic succession in it. A laying on of hands.

(After another pause)

I suppose there will be all sorts of stories set afloat by all sorts of liars when I am gone. And that's where you'll come in, Horace – to set the crooked straight. That'll be your time. And be sure you answer honest, so help you God. Whatever you do, do not prettify me. Include all the hells and damns.

HORACE

I promise not to help send you down into history wearing another man's clothes.

WALT

That's all I could ask, Horace.

(Pointing)

See that haversack on the wall? I want you to have it – put it among your treasures. That's a souvenir of the days when I was a nurse in the war.

(Horace takes down the haversack and hands it to Walt, who plays with it. Horace props himself up in the bed.)

I used it at that time in going about Washington – in the hospitals – among the soldier boys. Slung it over my shoulder in a way to make it comfortable. I used to spend every day and night in the hospitals a few hours. I always carried the haversack with the articles most wanted as I made my rounds among the boys – filled with things like homemade biscuits, some blackberry preserves, sometimes cut up a lot of peaches with sugar, plugs of tobacco, wine, brandy, pickles, letter-stamps, note paper, common handkerchiefs and napkins, socks, books, small sums of money, and fifty other things. I had lots of special requests.

HORACE

I'll put this in my Whitman gallery!

WALT

Oh, and there's a letter that goes with it. I was looking it over today – put it somewhere here on the top of the heap.

(He looks on the top of the pile)

Damn this mix-up! But I'm the chief mix-up myself – so why should I growl?

(He finds the letter)

Ah, here it is! One of my war letters – a hospital letter. The draft of a letter I sent to the parents of a boy who died. It was a pitiful, though after all, only a specimen case. They died all about us there just about in the same way – noble, sturdy, loyal boys. I always kept an outward calm in going among them – I had to – would have been useless if I hadn't – but no one could tell what I felt underneath it all – how hard it was for me to keep down the fierce flood threatening to break loose.

HORACE

Do you go back to those days?

WALT

I do not need to. I have never left them. They are here now while we are talking together – real, terrible, beautiful days! But now I want to hear Horace. Read! Read! My eyes are no good – I'm blind as two bats.

(Walt moves his chair closer to the bed while Horace reads. The image of the young man in bed and the poet by his bedside evokes the scene described in the letter.)

HORACE

(Reads)

"Washington, August 10, 1863

"Mr. and Mrs. Haskell, Dear Friends,

"I thought it would be soothing to you to have a few lines about the last days of your son Erastus Haskell of Company K 141st NY. I write in haste, but I have no doubt any thing about Erastus will be welcome.

"From the time he came into Armory Square Hospital until he died there was hardly a day but I was with him a portion of the time – if not in the day then at night. He was a quiet young man, behaved always so correct and decent, said little – I said once, jokingly, 'You don't talk much, Erastus, you leave me to do all the talking.' He only answered quietly, 'I never was much of a talker.'

"The doctor wished everyone to cheer him up very lively – I was always pleasant and cheerful with him, but never tried to be lively… I used to sit by the side of his bed generally silent, he was oppressed for breath and with the heat, and I would fan him – some days he dozed a good deal – sometimes when I would come in he woke up, and I would lean down and kiss him, he would reach out his hand and pat my hair and beard as I sat on the bed and leaned over him – it was painful to see the working in his throat to breathe.

"They tried to keep him up by giving him stimulants, wine, etc – these affected him and he wandered a good deal of the time – I would say, 'Erastus, don't you

remember me – don't you remember my name dear son?'
Once he looked at me quite a while when I asked him, he
mentioned over a name or two (one sounded like Mr.
Satchel) – and then he said, sadly, quite slow, as if to
himself, 'I don't remember, – I don't remember, – I don't
remember.' It was quite pitiful.

"For a long time previous, he was not well – didn't do
much – was in the band as a fifer – while he lay sick here
he had the fife on the little stand by his cot – he once told
me that if he got well he would play me a tune on it, 'but,'
he says, 'I am not much of a player yet.'

"Some nights I sat by his cot till far in the night in the dark
hospital. It was a curious and solemn scene, the sick and
wounded lying all around, and this dear young man close by
me, lying on what proved to be his death-bed. I do not know
his past, but what I saw and know of him he behaved like a
noble boy. I think you have reason to be proud of such a son
and all his relatives have cause to treasure his memory. He is
one of the thousands of our unknown American young
men in the ranks about whom there is no record or fame, no
fuss made about their dying unknown, but who are the real
precious and royal ones of this land, giving up, aye even their
young and precious lives in the country's cause.

"Poor dear son, though you were not my son, I felt to
love you as a son, what short time I saw you, sick and
dying there. These things are gloomy, but there is a text,
'God doeth all things well' – the meaning of which, after
due time, appears to the soul.

"Farewell dear boy, – it was my opportunity to be with you in your last days, – I had no chance to do much for you, nothing could be done – only you did not lay there among strangers, without having one near who loved you dearly and to whom you gave your dying kiss.

"Mr. and Mrs. Haskell, I have thus written rapidly whatever came up about Erastus, and must now close. Though we are strangers, and shall probably never see each other, I send you and all Erastus' brothers and sisters my love. I am merely a friend visiting the hospitals occasionally to cheer the wounded and sick.

"Walt Whitman."

(He looks at Walt with tears in his eyes)
This letter is alive all through – every word of it. It carries me back with you into that old experience, can see you there writing in the hospital and see the boys around you and smell the medicines –

WALT
I see that you understand it; well I understand it too. I know what you feel in reading it because I know what I felt in writing it. Horace, it was hard to hear that read. It is true – it is true. I can't live some of my old letters over again.

HORACE
These letters of yours to the soldiers are better than the gospel according to John for love – better than the Leaves itself.

WALT

Love – yes, that's the thing. Getting one and one together to make two. Getting the twos together and everywhere to make all. That's the only bond we should accept and that's the only freedom we should desire – love, love... Oh, Horace, I want you to keep it. I don't want to wipe out the memory. It is dear, sacred, infinitely to me – but I would rather not have it recur too frequently in the present condition of my body.

HORACE

Doctor Bucke says, "If Walt had stayed away from the war he would have been good for ninety years."

WALT

Yes – but there's more to the story. I never once have questioned the decision that led me into the War. Whatever the years have brought – whatever sickness, whatnot – I have accepted the result as inevitable and right. This is the very centre, circumference, umbilicus of my whole career... I suppose I should have been free of all this today if in those last years I had gone off to a place of safety, avoided the hospitals – taken special care of my own person – but here I am sick, nearly gone, and I do not regret what I did – it never occurred to me for a minute that there were two things to do – that I had any right or call to abandon my work with the soldiers. It was a religion with me...

HORACE
Religion?

WALT
Well, every man has a religion. Has something in heaven or earth which he will give up everything else for – something which absorbs him – which may be regarded by others as being useless – yet it is his dream, it is his lodestar, it is his master. That, whatever it is, seized upon me, made me its servant, slave – induced me to set aside the other ambitions – a trail of glory in the heavens, which I followed, followed with a full heart. I had to pay much for what I got, but what I got made what I paid for it, much as it was, seem cheap. I had to give up health for it – my body – the vitality of my physical self. Oh much had to go – much that was inestimable – that no man should give up until there is no longer any help for it – had to give that up – all that – and what did I get for it?… I never weighed what I gave for what I got, but I am satisfied with what I got… What did I get? Well – I got the boys, for one thing – the boys – thousands of them. They were, they are, they will be mine. I gave myself for them. Myself. I got the boys – then I got Leaves of Grass – the consummated book – the last confirming word. I got that. The boys. The Leaves. I got them.

HORACE
Walt, you gave up health, great as health is, for something greater than health.

WALT

Horace, that's what it means if it means anything! Oh
God! The whole damned war business is about nine
hundred and ninety-nine parts diarrhea to one part glory.
The people who like the wars should be compelled to
fight the wars. They are hellish businesses, wars – all wars.
Sherman said, war is hell – so it is – any honest man says
so – hates war, fighting, bloodletting. I was in the midst of
it all – saw war where war is worst – there I mixed with it
– and now I say,

(Rising up, shaking his fist)

God damn the wars – all wars! God damn every war! God
damn 'em. God damn 'em!

I shouldn't let myself go – no, I shouldn't – but I say God
damn 'em anyway.

*(After a pause he lifts his glass to the picture of Lincoln on the
wall)*

Here's to the blessed man above the mantel! After my
dear, dear mother, I guess Lincoln gets almost nearer me
than anybody else. He is like somebody that lives in our
own house.

HORACE

Did you ever see him yourself?

WALT

Yes, many times. Almost every day during the war we
passed each other on the way to our lodgings. We always

exchanged bows – and very cordial ones… remember one day so plainly – it was a reception day – there were crowds of strangers present, waiting their turn for a word with Lincoln. But Lincoln was engaged with an old friend – a minister who had come on from Illinois, was now talking to him. He was an old, splendidly preserved fellow – and bye and bye he had come upon the time to go, and Lincoln went along with him towards the door – as if loath to drop him – as if for old time's sweet sake he would continue the talk. Oh! –

(Bending his head sideways)
I can see him turned this way now – the ear bent down to catch the last word – the almost ungainly figure – the whole sad, strong, rugged, homely face lighted up. It was such incidents as these – I saw many of them – that revealed to me the real Lincoln.

HORACE
Do you have any pictures of him around?

WALT
Oh I have lots of them! I think I must at one time have collected fully fifty pictures of him. Most of them very cheap and hideous – as ugly as the devil. Yet beneath all the ugliness – under it – was an exquisite, fine, high nature – a nature too great for words – too intense for cold speech. One of the greatest, sweetest souls everyway.

(Looks around for a photo)

I'll give you one, Horace.

(He finds the photo on the floor)

It was here all the time. Of course, under a lot of other things!

(He looks lovingly at the photo, then hands it to Horace)

His ways were beautiful and simple. How well I knew them, watched them! And he was the same man in all relationships – for instance to the boys – the messenger boys – who came often – he would put his hands on their shoulders – say, "My son, is there an answer?" or "Sit down there, my son," something in that way, with a radiant kindness, humanity – in a natural tone, as if out of a great heart.

(Almost intimately)

No one can know better than I the preciousness of that gift to the age, to America!

(Pause)

I am getting to be a sort of monologuer. It is a disease that grows on a man who has no legs to walk on.

(He pours out more cider and they drink. Walt pins his quilt around his shoulders.)

HORACE

Walt, did I ever tell you about the time I met President Grant on a Camden ferry boat on his way back to Washington? He came up to me and asked me for the time, setting his watch by mine. Later I found my watch slow. I felt as if I had set the whole United States of America back.

WALT

(Laughing)

That's a good story boy – I can appreciate your remorse. But I have no doubts that you radical fellows have some theory that will set her right again!

HORACE

"You radical fellows?" Don't you belong with us?

WALT

Yes, yes I do – but not in whole and part. Sometimes I think some of you fellows have outstripped even me – have gone on even beyond me flaunting your red flag of revolt.

HORACE

Do you mean that for a rebuke or a blessing?

WALT

For a blessing to be sure. God bless the red flag of revolt!

HORACE

Did you know they are founding a Walt Whitman society in Boston?

WALT

Then God help me – I am lost!

HORACE

That won't be because you are lost – it will be because you are found.

WALT

How do you make that out?

HORACE

It will be a society of fraternity – of love without a creed. How does that strike you?

WALT

That might strike me, but it is impossible. There's a Sylvester Baxter – he's a theosophist and says I'm one. I had a letter from London the other day – from a young man. He says he's a socialist – then says I'm a socialist too. Tucker sees anarchism in the Leaves – sees me for an anarchist. So it goes.

HORACE

Every man thinks you are his personal fellowman, Walt. You are in the Plato class – the world class. You include all if you can't be included.

WALT

Do you say that knowing all it implies? Thank God! I hope I make room for all – include all – exclude nobody –

nobody whatever – shut no door. I don't intend it for cant when I say in my book that the best lesson is the lesson by which I myself am destroyed.

(After a pause, with playful exasperation)

Oh, no one can know what a center I am of the fancies of young and old – poets, writers, anarchists, communists, socialists, beggars, what-not. Everyone comes here demanding endorsements. A big lubber like me gets very little credit for being sick.

HORACE

Walt, do I come too much?

WALT

Does the fresh air come too much? Thank God for the fresh air.

HORACE

(Gingerly)

Does Anne Montgomerie ever come?

WALT

Yes, she comes sometimes – brings flowers – kisses me. But she doesn't come enough. When she was here last she brought me a bunch of roses, which were very beautiful, though she was more beautiful than her roses. She has cheeks like the prettiest peach in the orchard. You're always harping on her. What's Anne Montgomerie to you, or what are you to Anne Montgomerie, that you should love each other as you do?

(Pause)

A boy can do a lot sight worse than have a girl. He may not have a girl – that's a lot sight worse.

HORACE

And that from a bachelor!

WALT

Not too much of a bachelor, either, if you knew it all!

(Seriously)

Some time when you are ready and I am ready I will tell you the real story of my life. Then you will open your eyes.

HORACE

(Looking to see if Walt is smiling. He is serious.)

What do you mean?

WALT

I can't commence now – some day I will explain. I find it hard to steady my nerves for it – it means so much to me, will mean so much to you, means so much to others. I wish you on general principles to be made familiar with the one big factor, entanglement (I may almost say tragedy) of my life about which I have not so far talked freely... The cat has a long tail – a very, very long tail.

(Horace waits inquiringly)

Not tonight, Horace, dear boy – not tonight. Horace, you are the only person in the world whose questions I tolerate. I am not fond of questions – any questions, that is, that require answers. Even you at times, damn you, try me – but I answer your questions because you seem to me to have a superior right to ask them.

(Gaily)

Now, Horace, you see how much I love you. You have extorted my last secret. You have made me tell you why you are an exceptional person. You have forced from me an avowal of affection.

(After a silence, Horace gathers up his papers)

HORACE

Well – I must go now. I must not talk you to death.

WALT

I do not propose to die that way!

(Handing Horace a bundle)

Here, take this bundle for Burroughs to the post-office for me.

HORACE

And what about the wheelchair? Shall I go ahead with it?

WALT

I trust that to you – I leave it in your hands.

HORACE

And remember you promised never to go downstairs alone again.

WALT

Alright, I'll obey.
(Horace gets up to leave)
Kiss Anne Montgomerie for me, even if it is not lawful. Give my love to the boys. Tell them I dream of the ferry – of the water – of the wagons – everything – it all belongs to me. Tell Lindell at the ferry that I often think of him, as I sit here – of his damned old fiddle – I wish I could see him again – but my time is near, my time is near! And then there are all the fellows about everywhere to write to, keep in touch with them, for your sake, for mine. In all this world there's nothing so precious – in all this world, nothing.

HORACE

Goodbye, Walt!

WALT

No, Horace, I prefer goodnight. Goodbye is for all time, goodnight is for a little while.
(Horace kisses Walt)
Some night it will be a last kiss – last goodnight – but I hope not just yet – not till the book is done.

Horace departs.

PART II

About six o'clock in the evening,
May 31, 1891, Whitman's birthday

It is evening on Walt's birthday. Walt, dressed in his best gray suit, is sitting in a wheelchair looking out the window. His health has grown considerably worse. There are various gifts around the room, and doughnuts and champagne on the table. The room is tidier, but as the dialogue with Horace progresses Walt slowly reduces it to disorder.

WALT

I celebrate myself, and sing myself,
And what I assume you shall assume,
For every atom belonging to me as good belongs to you.

I loaf and invite my soul,
I lean and loaf at my ease observing a spear of summer grass.

My tongue, every atom of my blood, formed from this soil, this air,
Born here of parents born here, from parents the same, and their parents the same,
I, now thirty-seven years old in perfect health begin,
Hoping not to cease til death.

(While Walt is reciting his poem, Horace enters quietly with flowers and two books from the printer. Walt notices his presence.)

WALT

Is it a spirit? Why my boy, I didn't hear you at all.

(Noticing books)
What's that? What have you got there?
(Reaches for one of the books)

HORACE
Your birthday present, Walt!
(He hangs his hat on the bedpost and sits down)

WALT
Oh – it's more precious than gold – it's my baby book just born today – come safely at last through the great storm. Don't you see? I am celebrating two birthdays today.

HORACE
Well, where are your doubts now?

WALT
Gone, gone, gone utterly. I am completely satisfied – it is better even than I expected it would be. The book – the real, living, undoubted book!
(He turns the book over in his hand, inspecting it)
Horace – the deed is done. My blood, your blood went into the making of this book! Some men go to the North Pole to do things – some go to wars – some trade and swindle – we just stayed where we were and made a book. This is my birthday gift to the world – my last – my parting gift. The world has made many birthday gifts to me. A fair exchange is no robbery.

(Takes out book and writes on the flyleaf, repeating out loud)
"May 31, 1891: To Horace Traubel with the best memories and thanks of Walt Whitman."
(He gives the book to Horace)

HORACE
It's a victory!

WALT
This defied augury, it came out so fine. It's the best presswork I have ever had on any of my books. Horace, I want you to tell the fellows – the printer men – the publisher – all of them (don't forget the proof-reader) – that Walt Whitman is grateful for everything they have done – that he not only was – but is – one of them – that his pay is not the pay of money but the pay of love. Tell them that – tell even the flinty ones that. I want them to know that I am not in merely trade relations with them.

HORACE
I will, Walt.

WALT
(Tenderly)
Horace, how it happens you fall to my lot? There certainly was a divinity that shaped this end. How can I ever pay my debt to you?

HORACE
How can I ever pay my debt to you?

WALT
(Presses Horace's hand)
How can we?

HORACE
Let's pair off and say no more about it either side.

WALT
You have a way sometimes of settling my difficulties for me. Yes, let's pair off.

HORACE
It's easy for love to pair off.

WALT
It's easy for love to do miracles.

HORACE
(Handing Walt flowers)
I almost forgot – these are for you from Anne Montgomerie – out of her own yard.

WALT
The dear girl! Lilacs – Oh! How blessed! They seem right from God Almighty – are the most beautiful I have

ever looked on. Let's put them right here.

(Arranges the flowers in a glass, then pours water in the glass from a pitcher)

I've already had many letters today of congratulations – and three or four little remembrances.

(Showing cane)

This is one of my presents from Peter Doyle, my soldier friend – and three from Bucke: a bouquet of roses and two bottles of Jersey champagne. You see I am environed in riches.

HORACE

You take them very composedly.

WALT

Why shouldn't I? They are pleasant. We all like to be tickled – to be soft-soaped – we like to have our fur rubbed the right way… And by the way, that champagne – let's have some of it now – let's open one of the bottles. I've been patiently waiting a year for this.

HORACE

That's bad, Walt. They'll throw you out of the temperance society.

WALT

They can't. I never was in.

(Horace opens a bottle and pours some champagne; they drink and munch on doughnuts. He pours out another glass.)

HORACE
(Toasting)
Here's love for all the rest of your birthdays!

WALT
Here's love for the altogether beautiful people who have made me welcome on this earth.

HORACE
So, have you made an outing with your chair today?

WALT
Ah yes, it is just as if we were made for each other, this chair and me! Yes, I have been out – to my favorite companion – the river – was right down to the water's edge – the tide high and flowing strong – watched it as it flowed for a long while, a long while. It is a delicious going, resting – and the view over the waters – the big city there – the splashing ferryboats as they go! It was so fine! So full! I wanted to follow it over to the west!
(Pause)
But I have had a very bad day of it – very bad – all the symptoms of another spell – everything but the spell itself – but am better now, much better – since you came in and hung your hat on the bedpost.

HORACE
What's the trouble?

WALT

I am in a bad way. Belly, bladder, catarrh – my brain, physical brain – all are in – discomfortableation.
(Horace laughs, then Walt too)

HORACE

Let us call a doctor.

WALT

Don't get a doctor. I think of it this way, you know, that if the doctors come, I shall not only have to fight the disease but fight them.

HORACE

You are stubborn, Walt. Why don't you listen to us?

WALT

Of course you fellows will do as you think best – you do generally – I am in your hands. Yet I would have you always lean to the side of mercy – don't oppress me with doctors, nurses, medicaments. I am near enough dead as it is. No man housed up as I am could expect to hold his ground against old age. I do not hide the facts from myself.

HORACE

But that don't worry you. A man who isn't afraid of life isn't afraid of death.

WALT

(Fervently)

No indeed. I do not worry. I am not afraid. The fact that I am consciously staring death in the face don't make me less cheerful. Even death has its advantages – and death has its tomorrow.

(Serenely)

I like to think it over and over again with Epictetus – I have often said it to you, "What is good for thee, O nature, is good for me!" That is the foundation on which I build. It is the source of my great peace.

HORACE

Walt, Doctor Bucke thinks you have been pushing too strenuously with the book.

WALT

Don't you believe it! Not at all – not at all. It has been the best thing for me – has sustained me when everything else would have failed. As the sailors say when they are pretty sure of the harbor – we're going to fetch it! We've got past all, or nearly all, the dangers, headlands – our time is coming now – the voyage near done... Then you'll have to keep up the story alone.

HORACE

Well, that isn't here yet; we won't encourage it.

WALT

No, we won't. It was only a thought – a fleeting thought.
  (Pause)
There is something almost startling – or mysterious – that now, here, almost at my last day, there come all sorts of tributes from all sorts of men –
  (Pointing to the gifts and letters scattered about the room)
Friendly letters from Tennyson, Oscar Wilde, Mark Twain – requests for poems, invitations – Whitman societies – all converging to the one point of applause. They laud me to the seventh heaven – and to the roof of that! What does it mean? What? I am almost afraid of it!... O the mutations of years! Only a few years ago I waited for just such orders – but no message came – the world did not want me. Now comes a multitude – comes cry and cry – after I am wrecked, stranded, left but to look for the end – or near end! And yet there is a sense of satisfaction even in this – though how much of it is justified – who knows? Can it be a passing fashion?

HORACE

Suppose the whole damned thing went up in smoke, Walt, would you consider your life a failure?

WALT

Not a bit of it. Why my life? Why any life? No life is a failure. I have done the work. I have thrown my life into the work. In those early years in New York: teaching, loafing, working on the newspapers, traveling. Then in Washington: clerking, nursing the soldiers – putting my life into the scale – my single simple life – putting it up for what it is worth – into the book – pouring it into the book – honestly – without stint – giving the book all, all, all! Why should I call that a failure? Why? Why? I don't think a man can be so easily wrecked as that.

HORACE
You really mean that you don't think he can be wrecked at all.

WALT
Yes, that's better. That's saying the whole truth. Not wrecked at all.
  (A silence)

HORACE
Do you still have plans, Walt, now that the book is finished?

WALT
Oh, I am always scheming, surveying – putting in my stakes for new claims. I suppose I'll go on being like that until they nail down my coffin lid. I have just this morning mailed a short poem – a few lines – to Scribners. One more throw against oblivion.
  (Adding)

As long as I live the Leaves must go on.

(Factory whistles blow outside)

Six o'clock – the factory whistles – chimes.

(He wheels over to open the windows)

Between six and seven is the holy hour. The hour of the man who returns from work. The hour of the family, the table, the story, love, frolic. Oh how precious is that hour!

(Speaking to the men coming home from their factory jobs)

Hello, Danny. How do you do? Ha! Frank! Is that you? Say hello to Hannah for me – and to little Nellie! Tell her we are going to be great friends!

(A thoughtful pause)

Horace, what is your middle initial?

HORACE

"L." Why?

WALT

I propose making you my literary executor... You look surprised. Well, now you must behave!... First of all I want to protect Eddy – my poor stunted brother. Then I want to have this stuff round here taken care of. It would be all lost on my own family. There's not one of them who knows A from B in such things. I also want you to keep this for me –

(He hands Horace a document)

the deed to my lot at Harleigh's cemetery. You ought to go and visit – see the lot I selected – to me the most beautiful in the place. They wanted me to go in the open, in some prominent place – but I went deep in the woods!... Harleigh's offered it to me in exchange for a poem.

HORACE
That's a curious bargain.

WALT
I know it is, but now I am sure of a place to be buried in – if that has any importance.

HORACE
Some of the fellows wonder why you would wish to be buried in such a damned place as Camden.

WALT
What comes then is not to be worried over... I am most blessed in my Camden friends – all are kind, attentive, serve me... I came here years ago – in the first period of my paralysis – poor, weak, sick. The doctor warned me, "You'd better pack up and get out or, it'll be a coffin," so I put my stuff together and came to Camden. I saw this house on Mickle Street. It seemed to answer my purpose. Circumstances kept me here – bound me – here I am still.
 (Tenderly)
Horace, you were a mere boy then. We met – don't you remember? Not so often as now – not so intimately – but

I remember you so well. You were so slim, so upright, so sort of electrically buoyant. You were like medicine to me – better than medicine… Don't you recall those days? You would come along, I would be sitting there. We would have our chats. Oh, you were reading then like a fiend! You were always telling me about your endless books, books, books. I would have warned you, "Look out for the books!", had I not seen that you were going straight not crooked – that you were safe among books.

HORACE

Well, Walt – do you still think I go straight – that I am safe?

WALT

(Patting Horace's head)

You've gone from good to better right along. It'd have to be a damn crazy book to fool you. Why, Horace, I tremble in my boots for Leaves of Grass every time I see you open your eyes!

HORACE

Walt, do you remember the day you buried your brother, little Walter? How we met? How we walked a bit? How we had quite a little chat? How you took the car at Fifth Street? How we met again an hour or so later on the boat? I look back and see it all. You said, "Horace, it does me good – this air does me good – sort of makes me whole again after what I have gone through today."

WALT

(Trying to recall, finally stirring and exclaiming)

Yes! Now I do remember it! Not all the details you mention, but the circumstance, and I remember what maybe you have forgotten. That on the boat you bought some wildflowers from an old negro mammy who had been all day trying to sell them in the city and was going home dispirited. You bought her flowers and handed them to me. Do you remember that?

HORACE

Yes, now I do.

WALT

(After a pause, looking at his new cane)

Horace, did I ever introduce you to Peter Doyle – my soldier friend, a car-driver?

HORACE

No.

WALT

Well, we must arrange it some way some time. You and Peter would get to be great chums.

(Rummaging through a pile on the floor and picking up a photo)

I live here in a ruin of ruins. Look, here's a picture of us!

HORACE

(Reading the back of the photograph)

"Washington, D.C. 1865. Walt Whitman and his rebel soldier friend Peter Doyle."

(He mimics the sickly expression on Doyle's face)

WALT

Never mind, the expression on my face atones for all that is lacking in his. What do I look like there? Is it seriosity?

HORACE

No, fondness. And Doyle should be a girl!

WALT

Now, don't be too hard on him. He's my rebel friend, you know. You would like Peter – love him. Peter is a master character.

HORACE

One of your "powerful uneducated persons"?

WALT

Just that. A rare man, knowing nothing of books, knowing everything of life. A big rounded everyday working man full to the brim of the real substance of God. Dear Peter! Ah yes! – we would walk great walks together in the Washington days. Long, long walks, way into the nights!

And there were the detours too – wanderings off into the country out of the beaten path. How splendid above all, was the moon – the full moon, the half moon – and the wonder, the delight, of the silences… Many's the good day – night – we have had together!

HORACE
Don't you fear that your freedom with men may be misunderstood?

WALT
Do you misunderstand it?

HORACE
No. I see it for what it is. It is beautiful.

WALT
Misunderstood? Yes, it will be misunderstood. But what is there that I do that is not misunderstood.

HORACE
True! True!

WALT
The world is so topsy turvy, so afraid to love, so afraid to demonstrate, so good, so respectable, so aloof, that when it sees two people or more people who really, greatly, wholly care for each other and say so – they are incredulous

or suspicious, just as if they had somehow been the victim of an outrage. For instance, any demonstration between men – any – it is always misjudged – people come to conclusions about it – they know nothing, there is nothing to be known – nothing except what might just as well be known. Yet they shake their wise heads – they meet, gossip, generate slander. They know what is not to be known. They see what is not to be seen. So they confide in each other, tell the awful truth. The old women men – the old men women – the guessers – the false-witnesses – the whole caboodle of liars and fools.

(Playfully)

I am so opposed to respectability, they think I am not respectable.

HORACE

(After a pause)

You have not spoken to me yet of your great secret.

WALT

(Immediately growing grave, taking Horace's hand and looking into his eyes)

Yes, it belongs to you. You are entitled to know it. Some day. Some day soon.

HORACE

Maybe it's like the Diplomatic Secret, the secret being that there is no secret.

WALT
There is a secret. You will sometime see that there is a
secret.
(Horace waits inquiringly)
But not tonight, Horace, dear boy. Not tonight.

HORACE
Do you want me to stop asking?

WALT
No. No. I want you to keep on asking till I answer. Only
not tonight. Not tonight.
(Horace pours more champagne into Walt's glass)
Stop, Horace, that's enough!

HORACE
You only say that when the glass is filled!

WALT
Be good to me. I'm seventy-two today. Give me time to
straighten out the warps!
(Pause)
Did you know that I drank to the health of Queen Victoria
last week?

HORACE
(Irritated)
Why did you do that?

WALT

Well, I did! Took that big wine bottle from my table – drank good luck to the Queen's seventy-second year. Yes, indeed, did it with vim – and why not? My philosophy includes Queens too – though my friends got mad as fire with me when I did.

(Adding)

Anyhow let 'em kick. Kicking is good exercise!

HORACE

I bet the Queen would be surprised to find herself admitted into the inner circle!

WALT

Well, as the fellow did who unexpectedly found himself in heaven. He didn't ask himself whether he deserved it – he just kept quiet and stayed!

HORACE

(Looking around the room)

Speaking of heaven, it's so clean in here it looks like a Sunday school!

WALT

I was beginning to think maybe you didn't notice.

(Rummaging with his cane through the papers on the desk)

Order, order, everywhere, and not a thing to be found! Mrs. Davis cleaned up my room today.

(Motioning towards the several baskets overflowing with papers)
She arranged my things so I don't know where a damn thing is. Her heart is in the right place, though she has put everything in the wrong place.

HORACE
Have you any pictures of yourself around that I can have?

WALT
I have lots of pictures of me about here. No man has been photographed more than I have, or photographed worse. I've been photographed, photographed, photographed, until the cameras themselves are tired of me.
(He searches around, finds a photo and gives it to Horace)
Shall I help you out? Do you have this one?

HORACE
It has a rather ascetic look for you.

WALT
So it has, a sort of Moses-in-the-burning-bush look. It's a little rough and tumble possibly, but it's not a face I could hate. Could you? Honest injun, Horace, could you hate it?...
It was this I sent to Tennyson – and I heard he liked it well...

HORACE
Did you know Tennyson just said that he considered Walt Whitman the greatest of living poets?

WALT

Well, that is a feather in our cap, to be sure!

(Pause)

The big fellows are always the generous fellows. They recognize each other wherever they are. It will do for the little crowd to have all the bickerings, the mean jealousies, the quarreling ambitions. That's the way to distinguish the little from the big... I do not value literature as a profession. I feel about literature what Grant did about the war. He hated war. I hate literature. Literature is big in only one way – as a means whereby men may be revealed to each other as brothers.

HORACE

Walt, do you have hopes of me as a writer?

WALT

Oh, not only hopes – I am sure of you. I can't make out just now which road you will take, but you'll find a way and I have no doubt travel it with distinction.

HORACE

Once you said I was a damned fool – would never know how to write.

WALT

Did I say that? Well, I was a damned fool to say it. I can't imagine what could have tantalized me into such an outburst. You're still a pretty green pippin, but you'll ripen. After all, there's something better than to write – that's not to write. Writing is a disease. It'd be better if the whole tribe of the scribblers – every damned one of us – were sent off somewhere with toolchests to do some honest work. I believe if I met a man who had not written a book, I should hug him – he would be a monumental exception – an honorable exception.

HORACE
What I like about you, Walt, is that though you often talk strong you never talk sore.

WALT
I hope you are right – I hope you are right. But are you right?

HORACE
I haven't thought that today alone – I have thought it always. It is not a judgment for one day alone – it is for all time.

WALT
Thank God for that! Thank God for that! I would rather talk weak than talk sore. Thank God for that!

HORACE
You know, when I say radical things about you I get into a hell of a scrape.

WALT

Is that so, Horace, then why do you say the radical things?

HORACE

I can't help it. They sort of say themselves.

WALT

Take my advice – don't.

HORACE

But I can't. You are a disturber of public peace. You get your friends in trouble as the sparks fly upward.

WALT

(Stops sipping champagne and says seriously)
That is true. But don't you know what the scriptures say? "The son of man comes to bring a sword?"
(He resumes sipping champagne. A long thoughtful pause.)
The great thing with me is the spirit. As the old man said, my spirit is tremenjous – tremenjous. Thanks to myself in part, thanks in part to an occasional sip of champagne!
(Pause)
Horace, you know the day seized me powerfully yesterday, when I was down by the river, but I wondered why so few were out sailing. There was a good breeze, and yet the yachts were few. I am sure that if I had my legs and a boat, it would have been a day for me.

HORACE
And so to violate the Sabbath!

WALT
(Laughs)
No – I'd worship by it. Worship with the elements – with the water, the sky, the shore.

HORACE
Walt, that sentence is as good as a sermon.

WALT
Is that all it's worth? Is that the best you can say of it?

HORACE
You're an infidel, you'll be damned for your heresies.

WALT
I am glad to hear it! Glad to hear it! The company on the road will be large.
(More seriously)
And yet that is a queer notion – don't you think? As if we need to be damned anymore than to be the vermin many of us are at times! People have thought I was powerful "set agin' " the church, that it is a clean-cut bargain. I am done with the letter of the church, with its hands and knees – but that part of the church which is not jailed in church buildings is all mine too, as well as anybody's – all of it –

HORACE

But your whole book is religion. We do not want the figures for it. We are satisfied with the spirit.

WALT

Do you say that, Horace? But then you are always saying things! Well maybe – maybe. I never did feel as though the discussion of religion should be left to the priests; it never seemed to me safe in their hands. I am not convinced by the formal martyrdoms alone; I see martyrdoms wherever I go. The common heroisms of life are anyhow the real heroisms – the bits of brave conduct happening about us – the things that the preachers don't thank God for in their pulpits – the real things, nevertheless – the only things that eventuate in a good harvest.

HORACE

That's eloquent enough for congress and true enough for the Bible!

WALT

(Shaking his fist)

What do you know about either, anyhow? We talk about salvation. We need most of all to be saved from ourselves. Our own hells, hates, jealousies, thieveries. We need that salvation in the worst way. We seem to require all kinds of bigots to complete the chapter of our sorrows – Methodist bigots, Presbyterian bigots, the bigots for the bibles, the bigots against the Bible, Quaker bigots stiffer than their hats – all sorts – all sorts – we need them all to finish off the ornament of our hari-kari world.

HORACE
I'd like to see you in a pulpit once.

WALT
Once, did you say? Once? That's all it would be – I wouldn't last more than once – but I'd make all the fur fly while I lasted!
(Pause)
I ought to be saved in the end. I should say fifty or a hundred people are busy all the time trying to convert Walt Whitman from Leaves of Grass. Something ought to come of it all.

HORACE
(After a pause, looking out the window)
Look, it is clearing off. It is going to be a beautiful night.

WALT
(Wheeling over to see)
Oh, that is all gold there in the west!
(Wistfully, slowly)
It brings me back to my boyhood days on Paumonok – Long Island – standing barefoot, bareheaded on the shore – the sunset glow upon the waters – the fragrant sea-

breeze – the ocean rolling closer and closer. Some of my happiest hours have been spent there – some of my freest hours. They are past – gone forever.

(Pause)

I get very impatient some days. Wonder if it's all fair and square. Whether the scheme after all is not doubtful. Then I go back – find my way back to my central thought again – my spinal conviction – I resent my resentment – am ashamed of my questions. Oh, I feel how empty everything would seem if I was not full of this faith – if this faith did not overflow me! How useless all things would be if they led on to nothing but what we see – to nothing but what we appear to wind up in here.

HORACE
Walt, do you think we're led on and on to something that will finally satisfy us here or hereafter?

WALT
Yes.

HORACE
What?

WALT
I don't say what – I don't know what. I only say, to something. If I tried to prove things to myself I too would deny things. I do not prove things. I see! I see! I see! Seeing is enough.

(A silence, then sweet and graceful in gesture and expression)
I often think of myself – a living person – sitting here now – at seventy-two years – bridge across experiences, dangers, not to be computed. What a wonder it is –living still – living still – coming here out of the stages of babyhood. What more helpless creature is on this whole orb than the newborn baby? Yet I am here, held on and on – from that stage and stage, stage, stage, since. Is it not a wonder – a wonder?… In my periods of trouble – when I am sleepless – lie awake thinking – thinking of things I ought not to think about at all – am frustrated – worried – then I recover by centering all attention on the starry system – the orbs, globes – the vast spaces – the perpetual, perpetual, perpetual flux and flow – method, inevitability, dependability of the cosmos. It excites wonder, reverence, composure. I am always rendered back to myself.

(Wheeling forward and speaking from his deepest self as the sunset floods the room)

Splendor of ended day floating and filling me,
Hour prophetic, hour resuming the past,
Inflating my throat, you divine average,
You earth and life till the last ray gleams I sing.

Open mouth of my soul uttering gladness,
Eyes of my soul seeing perfection,
Natural life of me faithfully praising things,
Corroborating forever the triumph of things.

Good in all,
In the satisfaction and aplomb of animals,
In the annual return of the seasons,
In the hilarity of youth,
In the strength and flush of manhood,
In the grandeur and exquisiteness of old age,
In the superb vistas of death.

Wonderful to depart!
Wonderful to be here!

The heart, to jet the all-alike and innocent blood!
To breathe the air, how delicious!
To speak – to walk – to seize something by the hand! To prepare for sleep, for bed, to look on my rose-colored flesh!
To be conscious of my body, so satisfied, so large!
To be this incredible God I am!
To have gone forth among other Gods, these men and women I love.

O amazement of things – even to the last particle!
O spirituality of things!

I sing to the last the endless finales of things,
I praise with electric voice,
I say Nature continues, glory continues.
For I do not see one imperfection in the universe,

And I do not see one cause or result lamentable at last in
the universe.

O setting sun! though the time has come,
I still warble under you, if none else does, unmitigated
adoration.

(A silence in which they sit together affectionately)
We have had a beautiful talk – a beautiful talk.

HORACE
It's a Quaker talk.

WALT
That will describe it! But oh, how precious!
(Looking around for the bundle)
I put aside a bundle for you to mail to Doctor Bucke, but
now I cannot seem to find it.
*(He rises from his wheelchair to rummage for the bundle, and
then suddenly calls out)*
Horace! Horace! I must get to my bed – my head reels – I
feel as though a minute more on my feet – here would
finish me – be my last.
*(Horace springs to his side. Walt's head falls forward; he
seems about to faint; he reaches out and takes Horace's hand.)*
My cane! My cane!
*(Horace puts Walt's cane in his hand; Walt says nothing. He
tries to get up, resting his weight on Horace's shoulder. They*

*make their way to the bed and Walt falls back onto the pillow
exhausted, closing his eyes.)*
I'm a little shaken, but back on the throne.
(Pause)
Keep on your hunt, Horace – look for the bundle. When
you are done, turn the light down.

HORACE
Shall I go for Doctor Baker?

WALT
No! No! I need no doctor! I will be all right in a minute.
The doctor could do nothing for me. I have had fifty such
spells.
(He holds Horace's hand for a while)
Now I am easier – easier – much easier.
(Horace returns to search for the bundle)
Have you found it?

HORACE
(Finds bundle)
Here it is at last!

WALT
We lose, but we also gain!
(Horace begins to prepare his things for leaving)
Horace, take some of these doughnuts with you –
(Indicates doughnuts on the table)

– one for your sister, one for Anne Montgomerie, one for your mother. Mrs. Davis has been making them for my birthday – and we like to share a good thing when we have it. And tell them they are not doughnuts – tell them they are love.

(Horace takes the doughnuts)

HORACE
Goodnight, Walt!
(He kisses him)

WALT
And will you come tomorrow again! That everlasting, that sweet, tomorrow!

HORACE
Yes, take care of yourself till then.

WALT
Yes, yes. I'll be cautious. I'll come around by morning I know.
(Gravely)
All our goodnights are precious to me – and our good mornings.

(Horace turns down the light and exits)

PART III
*About six o'clock in the evening,
March 26, 1892, the day of Whitman's death*

Walt lies in bed propped up by a pillow. His eyes are wide open and facing the light. One foot juts out of the bed, resting on a chair. He holds a handkerchief in his left hand. During the dialogue, his words come out between coughs, with much effort, detached one from the other, but coherent. At times he cannot speak two words in one breath; he pulses them out at great cost. A fire is burning in the woodstove. The room is tidied a bit.

Horace enters, with a folio in his hand.

WALT
Ah Hor –
  (Chokes)
Horace?

HORACE
Yes! Another day gone.
  (He goes over to Walt's bedside, takes his hand that is lying on the pillow and clasps it)

WALT
Welcome, welcome! Another day! I thought I would see you this morning.

HORACE
You were asleep when I came in. The nurse was here.

WALT
I suppose. How is the weather?

HORACE
The snow is nearly all gone.

WALT
So soon?

HORACE
We touch the spring – the sun is warm!

WALT
The spring! Who would have predicted it? Is the room warm enough?

HORACE
Yes, Walt.

WALT
And is my body cold?

HORACE
(Stroking Walt's forehead)
Your head is quite warm.

WALT
Good, good! God bless you!
(Pressing Horace's hand)
What day is it?

HORACE
Saturday.

WALT

Last Saturday or next Saturday? Oh, I have lost the count!

HORACE

Do you feel any return of strength?

WALT

No, none.

HORACE

Loss?

WALT

Always – more – more.

HORACE

How are you feeling, Walt?

WALT

Like fifty thousand devils.
   (Horace laughs, then Walt, laughing and coughing at the same time)
I am going from one misery to another.

HORACE

I hope you shake off some of the pain.

WALT

It is pretty well over now, Horace.

HORACE
But you seem cheerful.

WALT
Do I? I hope so, especially as there's nothing else to be.
Now tell me the news, Horace.

HORACE
You have a great hunger for news. More than I can satisfy.

WALT
I suppose – but I have to get everything in brief – or not at all.

HORACE
I have had a letter from Burroughs.

WALT
With you?

HORACE
Yes.
  (Reaches into his pocket)
Can you stand it now or shall I postpone?

WALT
Read it now – now – now.

HORACE
  *(He takes out the letter and tries with difficulty to read it in
  the twilight. He lights a candle.)*
Does it hurt your eyes?

WALT

No – not a bit. Do not be afraid.

HORACE

(Reads)

"My Dear good old Friend,

"Just a line to you by tonight's mail to send you my love once more – the best I possess, along with my warmest sympathy.

"I hope you have had a good day and that your sleep tonight will be better than you have had of late. Horace continues to writes us every day and we send the letters on to all your other friends.

"Though I do not write much – for I fear to trouble you – my love knows no lessening.

"Good night to you, dearest and best of friends, and God bless you!

"Yours affectionately, John Burroughs."

WALT

(Interrupting in several places, stirred up, with tears gushing from his eyes)

Loving Burroughs! Dear Burroughs! Dear, dear good man! You are all good! We are compassed round by great loving arms, care, good will, the best.

HORACE

Do you hear it all?

WALT

Every word, every word – I am attentive to every word. It is a noble thought for Burroughs to send so warm a message at such a time.

HORACE

Walt, letters for you have come from all over the world, from all your friends.

WALT

The world is good of heart. I experience all the kindness of love – all the attentions, care. Everybody does me more than my due.

HORACE

Any messages for them?

WALT

No, none, I am emptied these days.

HORACE

Your love?

WALT

Always my love.

HORACE

Dave told me he sold six to seven hundred copies of the book since September.

WALT
Can that be possible?

HORACE
That is his statement.

WALT
Then we will have a little money next settlement?

HORACE
Yes, indeed – quite a block.

WALT
Good! Good!

HORACE
And he wants to issue a thousand more.

WALT
Yes, good, it will be alright; I leave it to you to settle with him. I leave everything I can for my brother Eddy – the poor, poor boy. Things have taken a turn for us – eh, Horace?

HORACE
And the reprint of "Good-bye My Fancy" arrived this morning.

WALT
How does the poem look? And the portraits? – what of them?
(Horace shows Walt the reprint of the poem and his portraits)

HORACE
Poor enough.

WALT
So I should suppose.

HORACE
The poem is one of your best – it is keyed way up.

WALT
You think so?
   (Calling out forcefully)
Horace – Horace – if I wrote anything more, I would speak about the way we have treated the death subject – based, absorbed in the natural. That that I've just said is quite a significant –
   (Breaking off, coughing)

HORACE
It is perfect in itself: one hardly needs to say more.

WALT
True, true – perhaps. But it will bear saying in full.
   (Suddenly, rallying his energy, Walt rises from his pillow, speaking almost vigorously, his eyes wide open, and lifting his hands)
All writings heretofore have been done on other suppositions – even Shakespeare's, Virgil's. But my own departure has

been quite definite and conclusive: and here, today, at the end, with the book closed, I glory in the surrender – have no regrets, have nothing to recall. It is by such unhesitating lines I have aimed to draw near the mysteries of nature: near them, to feel their breath, even when I knew nothing of what they meant, and could but wonder and listen, as if to vague music. I had all this clear from the start – I never erred – never strayed. And now, whether to be charged as a fool, or as reckoned victor, I am sure my choice, at least for me, was well-taken – was finally, the only path possible for me to foot.

HORACE
Yes, yes, Walt – I hear it all – I love it all.

WALT
Love it? Yes! And I loved it – oh, so much! – and now an end! But the book, Horace: there are things resting on you, too, to fulfill – many things. Keep a firm hand – stand on your own feet. Long have I kept my road – made my road: long, long! Now I am at bay – the last mile is driven: but the book – the book is safe!
   (Exhausted by the force of his utterance, he sinks back on the bed. After a pause, he asks quietly –)
Can you read it to me boy?

HORACE
Surely.
   (Reads from the folio)

Good-bye my Fancy!
Farewell dear mate, dear love!
I'm going away, I know not where,
Or to what fortune, or whether I may ever see you again,
So Good-bye my Fancy.

Now for my last – let me look back a moment;
The slower fainter ticking of the clock is in me,
Exit, nightfall, and soon the heart-thud stopping.

Long we have lived, joyed, caressed together;
Delightful – now separation – Good-bye my Fancy.
Long have we lived, slept, filtered, become really blended
into one;

If we go anywhere, we'll go together to meet what happens,
Then if we die we die together, (Yes, we'll remain one,)
May-be it is yourself now really ushering me to the true
songs, (who knows?)
May-be it is you the mortal knob really undoing, turning –
so now finally –
Good-bye – and hail! My Fancy.
   (Horace blows out the candle and puts the poem away)
It plays so grandly with its theme... with death.

WALT
Good! Good! So near port – in sight of port.
   (Horace kisses Walt, who presses his hand)
Horace – Bless you! Bless you! – you are always good to me.

HORACE
No – only as one having love.

108

WALT

Only as one having love. Anyhow, Horace, we are quite easy about that, which is enough.

   (They sit that way a while in silence; Walt is breathing hard.
   The factory whistles blow outside.)

That's six o'clock.

HORACE

Those are chimes.

WALT

I like them.

HORACE

   (Hesitantly, out of concern, not curiosity)

Walt… is there something you want to tell me?

WALT

   (Reflecting, then decisively)

Not tonight, Horace. Not tonight.

   (Suddenly)

Quick, Horace, I will have to be turned or I'll suffocate.

   (Horace turns him on his other side)

Oh-oh-oh-oh. Thanks – thanks. I seem to sink, sink, sink – yet never to reach bottom –

   (Pause)

yet – there is a bottom.

   (Crying in gasps)

Breath! Breath! Breath! Oh, lift me a little higher. Higher! Higher! The head! Lift! Good! Bless!

HORACE
You are very high now.

WALT
Well – just a little higher.
  (Horace lifts Walt's head higher)
That will do – yes that will do. Any change is so good!

HORACE
Walt, you're sweating!

WALT
Yes, dreadfully! – all over – wipe my face –
  (Adding with effort)
please.
  (Horace takes out a handkerchief and wipes Walt's face with it)
That's good.

HORACE
Your hands are cold.

WALT
No.

HORACE
Let me put a dry handkerchief on your neck?

WALT
Yes.
  (Horace does it)
Feels good.

HORACE

I am sorry that you must suffer so.
  (He holds Walt's hand until the end)

WALT

It's right. Bless. Bless.

HORACE

Is there anything I can do for you?

WALT

No – nothing – I have everything – nothing is wanting. You are all and everywhere kind and loving. No man could have more than that. Bless you always.
  (Calls out suddenly)
Shift! Shift!
  (Horace turns him; he breathes a sigh of relief and then soon after stops breathing. The canary delicately begins to warble. Horace leans down and kisses Walt's hand and head. After a long silence –)

HORACE

Goodbye, my fancy… farewell dear mate… dear love.
  (He puts his head down and quietly weeps, the canary's song filling the room)

WALT WHITMAN AND HORACE TRAUBEL

Walt Whitman was born May 31, 1819, the second of eight children. His early childhood was spent on his family's farm in West Hills, Long Island. When he was four years old, the family moved to Brooklyn. By the age of twelve, Walt left school, and began to work in the printing office of the *Long Island Patriot*. Afterwards he moved to the *Long Island Star*. He then made an attempt to found the weekly newspaper *The Long Islander* in 1838, which proved unsuccessful after one year.

In 1841, Whitman was in Manhattan working in the printing office of Park Benjamin's popular *New World*. It was during this period that he began writing poetry. He was able to publish some poems and prose in the *Democratic Review*. By 1842, Mr. Benjamin prompted Whitman to write a novel, and by November of the same year Whitman finished a work called *Franklin Evans; or, The Inebriate: A Tale of the Times*. Although Whitman dismissed the novel as an embarrassing melodrama, it became somewhat successful and would continue to sell as one of the best of all of his works during his lifetime.

During the early 1850s, Walt began developing his own free verse style. By 1855, the first edition of *Leaves of Grass* was published by two brothers under the family name of Rome. The Rome brothers graciously made the book available to give credence to the validity of Whitman's poetry. Whitman himself collaborated quite closely with the printing style. In a brief introduction to this original series of twelve poems, Whitman stated that Americans "have probably the fullest poetic nature" and that "the United States themselves are essentially the greatest poem."

The second edition of *Leaves of Grass* was published in 1856. It contained thirty-two poems. Whitman began to make his stand as a poet. He received high recognition from such prominent American poets as Ralph Waldo Emerson and Henry David Thoreau, who visited Whitman in Brooklyn in 1856. In 1857, he worked as the editor of the *Brooklyn Daily Times*. Two years later, he left this position and began once again to work on the poems for the third edition of *Leaves of Grass*.

In December 1862, Whitman received news that his brother George had been wounded at the battle of Fredericksburg. He immediately set off for Virginia with the sole intention of attending to his brother, but forthwith decided to remain. He was deeply affected by the unremitting suffering all around him, and wished to fully concern himself with the soldiers. He participated in the transport of many of these men from Virginia to the hospitals in Washington D.C. During the months that followed, Whitman would visit and revisit the sick and dying in the hospitals. He radiated an exuberant and positive aura that carried much emotional relief to this hellish world.

Whitman visited up to 100,000 soldiers during this period. He became their grandfather, mentor, friend, and confidante. The chief surgeon at the time, D. Willard Bliss, commented, "No one person who assisted in the hospitals during the war accomplished so much good to the soldier and for the Government as Mr. Whitman." He kept company with different boys during their horrific trials: whether physical – holding the hand of the soldier while undergoing a terribly painful operation without anesthesia; or psychological – bringing a compassionate note to the despair and disorientation of a young man facing his own death.

The years 1866 and 1867 witnessed various revisions of the *Leaves*. It was a volatile time, during which he was forced to grapple with censorship laws. In 1868, the first foreign edition was published by William Michael Rossetti, the brother of Dante Gabriel Rossetti. Fifteen hundred copies were printed.

On January 23, 1873, while at work, Whitman suffered a stroke that left him partially paralyzed. He was no longer able to work, and he moved to Camden, New Jersey to live with his mother and his brother. Three days later his mother died. This was quite difficult for him; a year later he was officially let go from his former position. Whitman was then forced to rely on his brother's financial support.

It was during this period that he and Horace Traubel first met. Horace was just under fifteen years old at the time. Walt became a mentor to the young Horace, and they would spend much time together meandering along the Camden streets, immersed in inspired conversations that sparked the young boy's love for literature.

Whitman looks back on their first meeting:

> Don't you recall those days? down on Stevens Street, out front there, under the trees? You would come along, you were reading like a fiend: you were always telling me about your endless books, books: I would have warned you, look out for books! had I not seen that you were going straight not crooked – that you were safe among books.

Neither Horace nor Walt ever could recall precisely the circumstances under which they first met. Their memories of earlier times only served to solidify the impression of a friendship that always had been.

In Horace, we find a character whose humanity soars far beyond the level of the simple interlocutor. We witness a young man whose strength of heart enables him to absorb Whitman's pain and lend buoyancy to the gravity of Whitman's illness. The simplicity and depth of their interaction, their reciprocal ability to bear the reality of a slow and continual farewell, gives breadth to an eternal and emergent friendship that goes beyond this little corner of history.

Horace Traubel was born in 1858. By the age of twelve, he had left school and apprenticed himself as a typesetter. His literary vocation sounded, he was carried through various jobs, each of which would help to refine his talent as a writer. Indeed, his middle name was Logo – an inscribed testimony on his very personae to the power of language.

During his early adult years, Traubel was able to bring Whitman's work to light in the realm of progressive political thought. Although Whitman would never have relegated his poetry and sentiment to any political and/or religious creed, Traubel had established himself as a point of reference in these circles, and as such brought credibility to Whitman's work.

Although the years that followed Whitman's death were marked with great hardship, Horace faithfully dedicated his life to the promulgation and prolonging of Whitman's literary heritage. He relinquished economic security, and his life took on the sense of mission not only in relation to Whitman but also to liberal/progressive social principals.

He spent much time reading, corresponding, and participating as America moved into the industrial age. One could say he lived the vital stream, the pulsing beat of Whitman's poetry within the context of his own lifestyle.

In June of 1917, he suffered the first of a series of heart attacks that eventually resulted in a cerebral hemorrhage. It was now 1918, just a year before the hundredth anniversary of Whitman's birth. Horace persisted. He was determined to greet this great occasion. On May 31st, he was able to attend a celebration in New York. There were two hundred Whitman followers on hand at this occasion, including Helen Keller, and he was given a standing ovation.

In August of 1919, Horace was at an estate in Canada called Bon Echo. He participated in the dedication of a cliff called "Old Walt" on which the following words are inscribed: "My foothold is tenon'd and mortis'd in granite/I laugh at what you call dissolution/and I know the amplitude of time." On August 28th, while looking out over "Old Walt", Traubel was heard to say that

Whitman revealed himself "in a golden glory." In Horace's words, "He reassured me, beckoned to me, and spoke to me. I heard his voice but did not understand all he said, only, 'Come on.' "

As Horace wrote in his last poem:

Well, Walt, here I am again, wanting to say something to you:
In a strange place, at the considerable north, talking again:
I just feel like as if I was having another chat with you as you sit in the big chair and with me in the bed opposite:
Oh! those blessed times, Walt! They're sacreder to me than the scriptures of races:
They're the scriptures of our two personal souls made one in a single supreme vision:
That's all for this moment, Walt: but it's the whole world of appearance and illumination, for all that.

Horace died on September 8th and was buried in Camden, near the tomb of Whitman.

Thomas Fenn